SLIDE A MIRROR TO ME

Poems by
ANNA KANDER

TRANSCENDENT ZERO PRESS

HOUSTON, TEXAS

© 2017 by Anna Kander

PUBLISHED BY TRANSCENDENT ZERO PRESS
www.transcendentzeropress.org

Cover design by Humbert Glaffo

All rights reserved. No part or parts of this book may be reproduced in any format, except for portions used in reviews, without expressed written consent from the author.

ISBN-13: 978-1-946460-97-4

ISBN-10: 1-946460-97-4

Printed in the United States of America

FIRST EDITION
Transcendent Zero Press

As she recovers from anxiety, a young woman training as a psychotherapist finds her studies complicated—then derailed—by attention from a teacher.

Called to counsel a girl who's attempted suicide, the woman must find a way to carry herself, and her lessons, forward…

Contents

Natural Light 7
Fingernails 8
The Body 12
To My Friend with Diabetes, On Losing Her Foot 14
Hydrangeas 17
Growing Up 20
Paper Cheerleaders 21
Lead 22
Arriving at a Shelter from Violence 24
Blue 25
The Sound of Metal 27
The Mermaid 30
Postcard from Red Riding Hood 31
Room Four 32
To the Bride 36
The Blue Whale 37

Acknowledgments 40
About the Author 43

Natural Light

The desire to be seen
transforms me.

Slide a mirror to me
under the door,
here in this dark room,
and I will find a way
to flash semaphores.

Fingernails

my psychotherapy teacher taught me to counsel
with his fingernails

to heal women in distress,
making first visits to trauma clinics,
by leaving space for them

to share as much—or little—of painful subjects
as they chose

by making statements instead of asking questions.

no demands, like
"We've just met—tell me your secrets."

no interrogations, like
"Do you hurt so much you can't breathe?"

instead I think aloud to myself,
as if I barely notice you in the room

"I wonder what it would be like to live through that."

a sentence, not a question mark,
voice not rising, ending soft and low

making silence

then inspecting my own fingernails—
palm up, fingers curled,
as if considering a manicure;

a deliberate inattention,

staring at my nails as if they were
the most interesting thing in the world;

giving space for a woman with wounds
to unwrap them, carefully,
without accidentally being touched.

fingernails—one aspect of a general posture:
self-contained and safe,

lower case,

never approaching, always reeling in,
letting her come to you.

we started in his office.

he let me watch him, and he watched me—
but only when he thought I was ready

(that I believe because I need to)

but we all have unconscious wishes,
and we all have tells

our tells can be funny—

every time he lectured me that
"clients have unconscious wishes,"
within the next twenty-four hours

he would offer to take my coat
or brush my hair from my neck
or some other small, inappropriate thing

learning by doing is treacherous.

teacher and student are not therapist and client;
there are not enough walls.

when he was finished with me,
there was another meeting, in another office,
and another statement instead of a question.

"I've taught with him, he's a good guy—
maybe you misunderstood."

at the meeting, a lawyer sat beside me,
picking at the beds of her nails,
her eyes misting the lenses of her spectacles,
hoping for my silence.

she'd warned, "It will be worse if you talk."

(yet here I am)

afterward, we sat outside, on a city bench,
its wood warmed by sunshine, in my hometown,
all the scenery looking changed.

when I looked down, I noticed her fists.
from her picked nails, blood ran down her fingers.

and

still, sometimes, I think of fingernails

memories
clawing at my back.

The Body

When I was 23, my brother introduced me to his corpse. After a ceremony at the medical school, he invited family to the hospital basement. We waited in a cool, dim hallway while he prepared the body. My mother grabbed my wrist, squeezing bones together.

"Ouch!" I said, and yanked my arm away to rub at invisible fingerprints.

"I'm here," she whispered. "Remember."

Inside the lab, the scent of formaldehyde stung my nostrils. My brother stood near a metal table where white sheets draped a human form. The subject for dissection was not overly large, only average, but fear made it massive.

"This is my body," my brother said. He peeled the sheet down, revealing a man's face and torso. The man was white, perhaps sixty years old, close enough that I could see pores on his face. The contrast between his waxen pallor and springy strands of hair made him look slightly fake, like a Barbie doll given a haircut.

My brother tucked the linens modestly and said words that were respectful. I don't remember them. "Natural causes," he added, "but that's not science. Sometimes we don't ask what happened, and sometimes we don't know."

As I looked at the man's face, my brother began to pull at a neat seam on his forehead. As smoothly as he had removed the sheet, he peeled back the man's scalp. It came away in a large flap—like a thick, curving orange rind. Then I saw the inside of his head.

My brother went from college to medical school, became a neurologist, and married a psychiatrist; each step took him further away. My path to becoming a counselor was less direct. It spanned five states, nineteen jobs, a broken foot—and two or three broken hearts.

(My tally is uncertain. How do you count a heart when it breaks, and breaks again?)

There is no tradition of healing in my family; we are starting something new.

I had nightmares about the body for a long time, but postmortems are how we learn. It's been four years since my brother stopped speaking to me. If we speak again, I'll ask about his dreams.

To My Friend with Diabetes, On Losing Her Foot

You walk sixty-seven years while childhood diabetes, against your iron will, poisons your peripheral nerves with sugar, and the muscles of your feet, starved of circulation, gradually dissolve.

Your toes gnarl and curl backward at wild angles, as if aspiring to adorn gargoyles. (You've always had a dragon-and-knight heart.) Unruly tendons draw themselves into bows, aiming toes in every direction.

The doctor calls nerve death a blessing: unmuffled shrieks of twisting bones, no one could stand. But nerve death isn't sudden, like cremation; electric signals climb your calves like flames.

First, you walk in special shoes; then, titanium braces, laced to your knees. Then, as orthotic specialists bite their fingernails, you cut holes in shoe leather with razors, because you have places no one can touch.

A medical resident offers custom replacements: braces with art printed on the back of your calves. You imagine the black-on-black silhouette of an animal whose feet don't have to touch the ground. You imagine a city to save. You say, "Batman."

Black on black is more than a side-eye at fate. You're making an all-season fashion statement: black shirts, black knee socks, elastic waists in cropped black pants to hold insulin pumps and air your knees.

(Your nerves still crackle like static.)

The new braces arrive. 1950s comic-book Batman, in a blue cape and a yellow belt, swings a punch and yells "Bam!"—because nothing turns out as we anticipate. At the checkout line in the grocery store, you become popular among small children.

Your toes still vogue, striking midnight poses, defying you to rein in their social lives. The doctor, that killjoy, assigns medical devices like curfews: each night, strap your soles to stiff boards and pull them toward your nose, to preserve the length of your tendons.

"No walking in night splints!" he instructs. Ha! The kitchen is all the way downstairs, and that's where the coffee pot lives, and you'd like to meet the hero who ties shoes without caffeine. The orthopedist surrenders, flips over your worn splints, and starts gluing treads.

Your tootsies are all-terrain vehicles, but the surgeons call them Charcot feet, after some French doctor. They translate: your feet are "bags of bones." Your grandchild mishears and begs to see your marvelous "shark-o" feet.

You blame the Discovery Channel, which hosts "Shark Week." You'd take a bite out of experts, all right. They have so much to say about science—and so little to say about the science of you. When you were twelve years old, they gave you insulin and pessimism. They said you'd never grow up—but you did.

You tower, and now they want to amputate. When the surgery is over, lean on me. I'm sending you into the operating room wearing a clean, white sock. On the sock—with a thick, black marker—I've drawn a face that smiles.

Sock, tell the surgeon that this woman is loved.

Hydrangeas

The snow-white hydrangeas will turn blue and fly into a million pieces, in a miraculous yet predictable process—almost science, but not what you'd think.

Through the thin lace of the kitchen curtain, I watch them—three-foot shrubs, planted by my mother, encroaching on the backyard. Nearby, two brown rabbits lounge, chewing dandelions, sucking juices from flower-stalk straws.

My mother, a gardener, meant well; but the only person I think of, when I spy those damn hydrangeas, is my sister-in-law—blue hydrangeas decorating the wedding, the day she took my only brother away. She grew up in a family that cut itself off from relatives, and I guess that tradition was her "something borrowed."

Don't bring a loving family to a broken one. It's like bringing a knife to a gun fight. None of us ever saw him again—and I hear that I'm an aunt.

*

In May, the lacecap flowerheads of the hydrangeas came in yellowish green, unfolding from their stems. In June, petals unfurled and rinsed in hard spring rains. The corymbs were brighter white than I could've dreamed—

Clusters of blossoms as big as white rabbits—baby rabbits, at least—newly washed, dried and cuddled, on sturdy green stems.

Or snowballs from hell.

Or polar-bear fists, clawing at my heart through my eyes.

*

My mother visits, sipping tea in the kitchen while I glare out the window at the hydrangeas.

Foolishly, I express relief. "At least the hydrangeas aren't blue."

That's when she mentions that, when she planted the unwelcome visitors, she dumped a bag of pine needles at the roots—to make the soil acidic. In time, the hydrangeas will turn blue.

Mother-effing blue.

Most hydrangeas stay white; a few in friendly, alkaline soil turn rose-pink. Only hydrangeas sprung from acid grow blue. How like my sister-in-law: a blue-countenanced perversion; the sad, visible result of an acid home.

My sister-in-law—adding acid, where I did not need any more color in my life.

My mother—always trying to fix things that do not need fixing, with pine needles or pleas.

I don't want to hurt my mother's feelings, or cut down her hope, so I will wait until after she dies. Then I will go into the yard with this kitchen knife and cut them from my sight, in a splatter of petals and weeping green stems—

and the real rabbits, brown-grey and blending with the earth, not stuck on green stems like party favors—

(and not effing acid-blue)

will enjoy a delicious meal.

Growing Up

What a disappointment
to realize the utter measure of men.

On the clocks of universes,
you towered for seconds.

Look down.
See your cartilage erode,
feel your discs flatten,
know your shrinking bones.

Each year, your up-righteous stances
grow more difficult.

Wobble across finish lines
and stand on shards.

Paper Cheerleaders

fair-weather friends—

cut-out paper dolls unfolding
from white paper

cheering triumphs atop pyramids

overlooking sturdy shoulders
and bruising practice falls

you start to look the same
row after row

flat and colorless
strung between triangles of air—

pieces of you, missing
that harsh hands snipped away

crinkling and wavering
i see through you

i want to crumple you
pile you in the corner, without care

as missed shots at the wire basket
beneath my desk

because i have other shots to take
with more weight

than paper

Lead

My world snapped like pencil lead, sliding from its wooden barrel during a must-pass test.

(probably I push too hard)

The wood fell away, a useless shell. Left was a stub of graphite which I sheltered, cupping my hands and pressing them to the desk.

Panic! Post-pencil apocalypse seemed a barren hellscape, littered with broken pencil sharpeners. There were no level surfaces—everything skewed.

The danger was acute. I imagined the sliver of silver rolling from the desk—falling—plummeting to an abyss of cracked floor tiles.

(bless the parentheses of my hands, protecting)

Then—the test caught fire.

This wasn't a dream. This wasn't a drill.

Flames leapt from the instructions. Their white-orange tongues purpled, tasting potassium in the paper.

As the desktop laminate grew hot and gluey, my answers blackened from edges to centers. They curled into ash.

I don't try to explain it anymore—the pencil snap or the fire. Some disasters have no predicting—and no avoiding.

Sometimes these things just happen.

After the fire, passion seized me. With more feeling for my puny, imperfect instrument than I'd ever expected, I plucked that sliver of graphite from the desk and held it

(softly)

between my forefinger and thumb.

I wrote with the nub, and I colored with the ash. Everything became my canvas.

Arriving at a Shelter from Violence

Your wounds are fresh
and still too deep
to paint your surfaces blue.

Only pinpoints of blood
decorate your skin,
like freckles on little girls
before we train them
to blush, gloss,
conceal.

The red dots are petechiae,
and I connect them.
Blood spills from your capillaries,
the last destinations of your cardiovasculature,
the furthest reaches of your heart.

Sit with me,
and I will hold your hand
until strangers no longer stare and judge,
until the bruises bloom
and fade,

and you remain.

Blue

Ladies and gentlemen, place your bets!

Blue-chip companies take their name from the color of the highest-valued chips at poker tables on October 28, 1929.

(we're reliable, all-American, safe)

Then comes October 29, 1929: the day the stock markets crash.

Then comes October 30, 2009: me, new to a minimum-wage custodial crew, learning that the most important thing, when you clean the headquarters of a multibillion-dollar corporation, is the executive washroom.

The questions are not: Are floors swept? Are counters and toilets clean?

The real questions are: Is the trash empty, even if there were only three paper towels in the bin?

(they don't want to see trash)

Did you wipe away any fingerprints left when you opened the shiny chrome stall doors?

(they want you to be invisible)

And is the water in the toilet bowl a reassuring, disinfectant-blue?

No? We've no time. They don't pay us enough to stay any longer. Night janitors got to hustle to the next job.

Just spritz some blue in there, let's go.

(they don't want to see)

(they'll never know)

The Sound of Metal

love your brothers and sisters, momma said
carry us like a song in your heart

in high school, i whispered gossip to mean girls
and, on alternate Tuesdays, tried to not to drown

in labels
and expectations

and a labyrinth of dented lockers
that made hollow sounds

when bodies and metal collided
for the thousandth occasion

at the same high school
at the same time

my brother was molested

we didn't learn what happened 'til years later
after he stopped coming home

on a field trip with an overnight bus ride
two rich boys—also brothers
pinned him in the corner of the high, stiff seat
used some sort of hard implement

one of them held a knife
it scraped the metal frame around the window

screeching metal around a black night
swallowing all those stars

anyway, that's what I heard
third-hand, from our mother

or fourth- or fifth-hand, if i am counting
the rich brothers

in English, there are at least nineteen words
to describe the sounds of metal

clang, ding, clatter, clunk, clash
drum, echo, jangle, rattle, rasp

jingle, gong, plink, tinkle
                        crash

wood blocks make dull thumps

strike metal and it sings
releasing sounds sharp like weapons
for avenging

the energy of struck metal dissipates gradually
scientists say that's because metal is "elastic"
i'd say metal remembers

the oscillations of metal decay slowly
my brother went silent; the metal still screams

every autumn, as purple and gold leaves fall
from the copper beech and sugar maples

my brothers and sisters who can travel
return to visit our small town

migrating back to the place of our birth, like salmon
lively until we are made someone's dinner

we will clink forks and knives on the good china
and enjoy a ritual meal

we had all our friends in common
and I will see them

when I run to the drugstore for shampoo and chocolates
pieces of home that I forgot to bring

tokens of appreciation that somehow slip my mind
every single goddamn year

your friends from high school will ask me about you again
and I'll say no, he won't be coming home

no, he won't be here
for thanksgiving

The Mermaid

she flashed a lower limb at us
splashing partly out of the water

breaking the surface
of our romantic notions

she didn't have the tail we expected
the magic

instead she pressed her thighs together
closing off half of herself

flipping through the water
a thousand miles from shore

beautiful, but not ageless
aging

not a woman born to water
buoyant in tears

but heavy with effort
and mending bones

a survivor of wreckage
a woman who remembered land

Postcard from Red Riding Hood, that little girl who used to live next door

"Still climbing in bed with wolves."

Room Four

Alice is the youngest girl in Room Four. I, the woman eldest. She misses part of the fall when she goes into the hospital, suicidal.

I commute hundreds of miles to the counseling school where I'll finish training. My job supports me, though bosses probably guess that I've left the first school after scandal.

(teacher student teacher)

The old teacher was too close. The new school is too far. Everything is a matter of distances.

The old school battens hatches, but I jam my foot in the last closing door. Instead of my final class in counseling, I take my first class in creative writing—Building B, Room Four.

At last, Alice returns.

She bares her bright scars to the class, in a group notice like a wedding invitation or a graduation announcement.

She says, "I had to tell my roommates."

Later, she reveals that she was raped.

Alice is slight, thin and small; even her skull seems delicate. Her hair evolves: from a dark mohawk to a bleached mohawk, tipped Barbie pink.

The day Alice scoots her desk toward me, across the long room, the mohawk is gone. Her hair is shorn to a spiky brown cap that shines like an otter's pelt.

"Read your drafts to each other," the teacher says. "Hear your story from someone else."

"It's a draft until you lift the pen," she says. "It's a draft until you're dead."

A week after Alice returns from the hospital, I email all seven "Alices" in the directory. "I'm glad you felt safe to tell us," I write. "If you need me, I'm here."

"Class" Alice doesn't answer. Another Alice does. "I'm so sorry," she writes back. "I'm not the person you're looking for."

In class, Alice draws her desk to me and smooths papers beneath her fingers.

"I've never shared this with anyone," she says. "You're the first person to read this."

She hands me a thick, spiral notebook—it weighs in my hands.

There are instructions for reading.

Alice turns past class notes, opening her book to the last page. She shows me the last page, front and back, then shows me the second-from-last page.

"Read one, then two," she says. "Three, then four. This is how I write."

From Alice, I learn to look. At first, her book seemed a stretch of blank pages. "Stop! There's nothing to see." We hide stories behind paper fortresses.

I begin.

The text is new. I do my best to honor it with resonant speech and pauses, breathing life into fantastical places and names.

Parents are gods.

(teachers are gods)

Children, rescued, are wolves who sometimes grow into men.

It's a telling of Romulus and Remus.

Alice's handwriting is printed in pencil, a childlike scrawl littered with spelling mistakes. I step through each with purpose, not-noticing. She corrects me when I guess wrong.

There are no eraser marks.

At page four, I look at Alice for permission to continue. She nods, and I turn to page five.

There are many ways to do the caring that is counseling.

(teacher student teacher)

When classes began, Alice filled our discussions. She could talk sixty minutes in three hours. With cautious encouragement from the teacher, she has grown silent.

"This is the start of a longer story," Alice says. "I'm not finished."

I hold the paper delicately, at its edges, careful not to smudge.

To the Bride

Each god, he weakens your knees
but flees from trouble.

Anchor him to an altar.
Anchor him to your own church.

In a thicket of embraces
enough to clip women in half,
you will have to be killing-strong.

Widow, rise up.

Rip into the world with your teeth.

You are the revenant,
the heart that remains.
Clench every unpredictable beat.

You are a survivor with limited rations,
not enough left to keep blind rule-following alive—
hard choices to be made.

First, start the bonfire with your rage,
incinerating the old life.

Find a way to make peace
enough with the world to stay in it,
to make room for yourself—and others.

Build a new house; shelter us.
Pierce the sky with your steeple
and throw open the doors.

The Blue Whale

my creative spirit
is a blue whale, I think

she swims in deep waters
but we breathe the same air

and, like other blue whales,
she has the loudest, strongest voice on earth

which is fortunate (thank the earth)
because if there is a second voice

she's a howler monkey—
loud, too, and rather obnoxious

that's perfection, the crank upstairs
I've tried to evict, but she just won't leave

she runs a lighthouse
illuminating the goal but not the path

through dark, choppy waters
to where I aim but never land

always at sea

(thank the stars) my spirit is part whale
and I can dwell among those who don't reach

all the shining high lights
or the shores they seek

despite all that double-edged help from
howler monkeys in lighthouses

(thank the sea)

I breathe just fine down here.

The End

Acknowledgments

Thank you to C, J, R, and S. Without you, this book would not exist.

Thank you to everyone at Absolute Write and 51 Writers who helped me by beta reading, cheering, teaching me about publishing, and sharing their general awesomeness.

Thank you to the journals that first printed versions of the following poems: "Arriving at a Shelter from Violence" first appeared in *Ariel Chart*. "Blue" first appeared in *Faded Out*. "The Blue Whale" first appeared in *Dear Damsels*. "Fingernails" first appeared in *Gone Lawn*. "Growing Up" first appeared in *Leveler*. "Hydrangeas" first appeared in *Ellipsis*. "Lead" first appeared in *Train*. "The Mermaid" first appeared in *Smeuse*. "Natural Light" first appeared in *Gnarled Oak*. "Paper Cheerleaders" first appeared in *Wanton Fuckery*. "Postcard from Red Riding Hood" first appeared in *Literary Juice*. "Room Four" first appeared in *Five on the Fifth*. "The Sound of Metal" first appeared in *Degenerates: Voices for Peace*. "To My Friend with Diabetes, On Losing Her Foot" first appeared in *Hektoen International*. "To the Bride" first appeared in *Barking Sycamores*.

Thank you to Dustin and Transcendent Zero Press for publishing this book.

Thank you for reading! If you enjoyed the book, I'd appreciate a review on Amazon or Goodreads—reviews help other readers find books they might enjoy.

You can also find me at my website, annakander.com. There you can leave feedback, read new poems and stories, or subscribe to receive an email when my next book is published.

Please watch for my forthcoming novel, *The Ripped Heart*.

—Anna Kander
November 2017

About the Author

Anna Kander is a writer in the Midwest. She trained as a psychotherapist and remains licensed to practice. She writes with her sidekick, a fearless blue fish who doesn't realize he's only one inch tall. Her poetry and stories have appeared in *Gnarled Oak, Social Justice, Dear Damsels,* and other journals.

You can learn more at…

Website annakander.com
Twitter @annakander
Facebook.com/annakanderwrites
Goodreads.com/anna_kander

Praise for *Slide a Mirror to Me*

"Heartbreaking in places, and beautiful."

—Heather Kinnane, romance author

"Raw and emotional. Anna Kander has created a collection of poetry that anyone can relate to—and enjoy."

—Anne Wheeler, author of *Forever's End*

"More women should have loud and obnoxious creative spirits, telling us not to shut up, telling us not to give up, making us be loud and obnoxious too."

—Dr. Sara L. Uckelman, author and Assistant Professor of Philosophy, Durham University

"There's anger in the speaker's voice… it's a truth that is hard to express in any other way. A more forgiving voice would be self-defeating. A more ambiguous take belongs somewhere else."

—Yotam Hadass, Editor, *Leveler Poetry*

"Anna Kander's poignant and often playful poetry throws light on some dark and difficult areas and, with its unshouty tone, reels us in."

—Beth Somerford, Editor, *Smeuse Poetry*

www.ingramcontent.com/pod-product-compliance
Lightning Source LLC
Chambersburg PA
CBHW061306040426
42444CB00010B/2544